George Meredith

An Essay on Comedy and the Uses of the Comic Spirit

George Meredith

An Essay on Comedy and the Uses of the Comic Spirit

ISBN/EAN: 9783744770866

Printed in Europe, USA, Canada, Australia, Japan

Cover: Foto ©Thomas Meinert / pixelio.de

More available books at **www.hansebooks.com**

AN ESSAY ON

COMEDY

AND THE USES OF THE

COMIC SPIRIT

BY

GEORGE MEREDITH

NEW YORK
CHARLES SCRIBNER'S SONS
1897

𝔘niversity 𝔓ress :

JOHN WILSON AND SON, CAMBRIDGE, U.S.A.

AN ESSAY
ON COMEDY

ON THE IDEA OF COMEDY AND OF THE USES OF THE COMIC SPIRIT [1]

Good Comedies are such rare productions, that notwithstanding the wealth of our literature in the Comic element, it would not occupy us long to run over the English list. If they are brought to the test I shall propose, very reputable Comedies will be found unworthy of their station, like the ladies of Arthur's Court when they were reduced to the ordeal of the mantle.

There are plain reasons why the Comic poet is not a frequent apparition; and why the great Comic poet remains without a

[1] A lecture delivered at the London Institution, February 1st, 1877, and afterwards published in 'The New Quarterly Magazine' for April, 1877.

1

fellow.   A society of cultivated men and women is required, wherein ideas are current and the perceptions quick, that he may be supplied with matter and an audience.   The semi-barbarism of merely giddy communities, and feverish emotional periods, repel him; and also a state of marked social inequality of the sexes; nor can he whose business is to address the mind be understood where there is not a moderate degree of intellectual activity.

Moreover, to touch and kindle the mind through laughter, demands more than sprightliness, a most subtle delicacy.   That must be a natal gift in the Comic poet.   The substance he deals with will show him a startling exhibition of the dyer's hand, if he is without it. People are ready to surrender themselves to witty thumps on the back, breast, and sides; all except the head: and it is there that he aims.   He must be subtle to penetrate.   A corresponding acuteness must exist to welcome him.   The necessity for the two conditions will explain how it is that we count him during centuries in the singular number.

'C'est une étrange entreprise que celle de faire rire les honnêtes gens,' Molière says; and the difficulty of the undertaking cannot be over-estimated.

Then again, he is beset with foes to right and left, of a character unknown to the tragic and the lyric poet, or even to philosophers.

We have in this world men whom Rabelais would call agelasts; that is to say, non-laughers; men who are in that respect as dead bodies, which if you prick them do not bleed. The old grey boulder-stone that has finished its peregrination from the rock to the valley, is as easily to be set rolling up again as these men laughing. No collision of circumstances in our mortal career strikes a light for them. It is but one step from being agelastic to misogelastic, and the μισό-γελως, the laughter-hating, soon learns to dignify his dislike as an objection in morality.

We have another class of men, who are

pleased to consider themselves antagonists of the foregoing, and whom we may term hyper-gelasts; the excessive laughers, ever-laughing, who are as clappers of a bell, that may be rung by a breeze, a grimace; who are so loosely put together that a wink will shake them.

'. . . C'est n'estimer rien qu'estimer tout le monde,'

and to laugh at everything is to have no appreciation of the Comic of Comedy.

Neither of these distinct divisions of non-laughers and over-laughers would be enter-tained by reading The Rape of the Lock, or seeing a performance of Le Tartuffe. In relation to the stage, they have taken in our land the form and title of Puritan and Bacchanalian. For though the stage is no longer a public offender, and Shakespeare has been revived on it, to give it nobility, we have not yet entirely raised it above the contention of these two parties. Our speaking on the theme of Comedy will appear almost a libertine proceeding to one, while the other will think that the speaking of it seriously brings us into violent contrast with the subject.

Comedy, we have to admit, was never one of the most honoured of the Muses. She was in her origin, short of slaughter, the loudest expression of the little civilization of men. The light of Athene over the head of Achilles illuminates the birth of Greek Tragedy. But Comedy rolled in shouting under the divine protection of the Son of the Wine-jar, as Dionysus is made to proclaim himself by Aristophanes. Our second Charles was the patron, of like benignity, of our Comedy of Manners, which began similarly as a combative performance, under a licence to deride and outrage the Puritan, and was here and there Bacchanalian beyond the Aristophanic example: worse, inasmuch as a cynical licentiousness is more abominable than frank filth. An eminent Frenchman judges from the quality of some of the stuff dredged up for the laughter of men and women who sat through an Athenian Comic play, that they could have had small delicacy in other affairs when they had so little in their choice of entertainment. Perhaps he does not make sufficient allowance for the regulated licence of plain speaking proper to the festival of the god, and claimed by the Comic poet as his inalienable right, or for the fact that it was a festival in a season of licence, in a city accustomed to give ear to the boldest utterance of both sides of a case. However that may be, there can be no question that the men and women who sat through the acting of Wycherley's Country Wife were past blushing. Our tenacity of national impressions has caused the word theatre since then to prod the Puritan nervous system like a satanic instrument; just as one has known Anti-Papists, for whom Smithfield was redolent of a sinister smoke, as though they had a later recollection of the place than the lowing herds. Hereditary Puritanism, regarding the stage, is met, to this day, in many families quite undistinguished by arrogant piety. It has subsided altogether as a power in the profession of morality; but it is an error to suppose it extinct, and unjust also to forget that it had once good reason to hate, shun, and rebuke our public shows.

We shall find ourselves about where the Comic spirit would place us, if we stand at middle distance between the inveterate opponents and the drum-and-fife supporters of Comedy: 'Comme un point fixe fait remarquer l'emportement des autres,' as Pascal says. And were there more in this position, Comic genius would flourish.

Our English idea of a Comedy of Manners might be imaged in the person of a blowsy country girl — say Hoyden, the daughter of Sir Tunbelly Clumsy, who, when at home, 'never disobeyed her father except in the eating of green gooseberries' — transforming to a varnished City madam; with a loud laugh and a mincing step; the crazy ancestress

of an accountably fallen descendant. She
bustles prodigiously and is punctually smart
in her speech, always in a fluster to escape
from Dulness, as they say the dogs on the
Nile-banks drink at the river running to avoid
the crocodile. If the monster catches her, as
at times he does, she whips him to a froth,
so that those who know Dulness only as a
thing of ponderousness, shall fail to recognise
him in that light and airy shape.

When she has frolicked through her five
Acts to surprise you with the information
that Mr. Aimwell is converted by a sudden
death in the world outside the scenes into
Lord Aimwell, and can marry the lady in
the light of day, it is to the credit of her
vivacious nature that she does not anticipate
your calling her Farce. Five is dignity with
a trailing robe; whereas one, two, or three
Acts would be short skirts, and degrading.
Advice has been given to householders, that
they should follow up the shot at a burglar
in the dark by hurling the pistol after it,

so that if the bullet misses, the weapon may strike and assure the rascal he has it. The point of her wit is in this fashion supplemented by the rattle of her tongue, and effectively, according to the testimony of her admirers. Her wit is at once, like steam in an engine, the motive force and the warning whistle of her headlong course; and it vanishes like the track of steam when she has reached her terminus, never troubling the brains afterwards; a merit that it shares with good wine, to the joy of the Bacchanalians. As to this wit, it is warlike. In the neatest hands it is like the sword of the cavalier in the Mall, quick to flash out upon slight provocation, and for a similar office — to wound. Commonly its attitude is entirely pugilistic; two blunt fists rallying and countering. When harmless, as when the word 'fool' occurs, or allusions to the state of husband, it has the sound of the smack of harlequin's wand upon clown, and is to the same extent exhilarating. Believe that idle empty laughter is the most desirable of recreations, and significant Comedy will seem pale and shallow in comparison. Our popular idea would be hit by the sculptured group of Laughter holding both his sides, while Comedy pummels, by way of tickling him. As to a meaning, she holds that it does not conduce to making merry : you might as well carry cannon on a racing-yacht. Morality is a duenna to be circumvented. This was the view of English Comedy of a sagacious essayist, who said that the end of a Comedy would often be the commencement of a Tragedy, were the curtain to rise again on the performers. In those old days female modesty was protected by a fan, behind which, and it was of a convenient semicircular breadth, the ladies present in the theatre retired at a signal of decorum, to peep, covertly askant, or with the option of so peeping, through a prettily fringed eyelet-hole in the eclipsing arch.

' Ego limis specto sic per flabellum clanculum.'—

TERENCE.

That fan is the flag and symbol of the society giving us our so-called Comedy of Manners, or Comedy of the manners of South-sea Islanders under city veneer; and as to Comic idea, vacuous as the mask without the face behind it.

Elia, whose humour delighted in floating a galleon paradox and wafting it as far as it would go, bewails the extinction of our artificial Comedy, like a poet sighing over the vanished splendour of Cleopatra's Nile-barge; and the sedateness of his plea for a cause condemned even in his time to the penitentiary, is a novel effect of the ludicrous. When the realism of those 'fictitious half-believed personages,' as he calls them, had ceased to strike, they were objectionable company, uncaressable as puppets. Their artifices are staringly naked, and have now the effect of a painted face viewed, after warm hours of dancing, in the morning light. How could the Lurewells and the Plyants ever have been praised for ingenuity in wickedness? Critics,

apparently sober, and of high reputation, held
up their shallow knaveries for the world to
admire.   These Lurewells, Plyants, Pinch-
wifes, Fondlewifes, Miss Prue, Peggy, Hoyden,
all of them save charming Millamant, are dead
as last year's clothes in a fashionable fine
lady's wardrobe, and it must be an exception-
ably abandoned Abigail of our period that
would look on them with the wish to appear
in their likeness.   Whether the puppet show
of Punch and Judy inspires our street-urchins
to have instant recourse to their fists in a
dispute, after the fashion of every one of the
actors in that public entertainment who gets
possession of the cudgel, is open to question:
it has been hinted; and angry moralists have
traced the national taste for tales of crime
to the smell of blood in our nursery-songs.   It
will at any rate hardly be questioned that it
is unwholesome for men and women to see
themselves as they are, if they are no better
than they should be: and they will not, when
they have improved in manners, care much to

see themselves as they once were. That comes
of realism in the Comic art; and it is not
public caprice, but the consequence of a bet-
tering state.[1] The same of an immoral may
be said of realistic exhibitions of a vulgar
society.

The French make a critical distinction in
ce qui remue from *ce qui émeut* — that which
agitates from that which touches with emo-
tion. In the realistic comedy it is an incessant
remuage — no calm, merely bustling figures,
and no thought. Excepting Congreve's Way
of the World, which failed on the stage, there
was nothing to keep our comedy alive on its
merits; neither, with all its realism, true por-
traiture, nor much quotable fun, nor idea;
neither salt nor soul.

The French have a school of stately comedy
to which they can fly for renovation whenever
they have fallen away from it; and their

---

[1] Realism in the writing is carried to such a pitch
in *The Old Bachelor*, that husband and wife use imbecile
connubial epithets to one another.

having such a school is mainly the reason
why, as John Stuart Mill pointed out, they
know men and women more accurately than
we do. Molière followed the Horatian pre-
cept, to observe the manners of his age and
give his characters the colour befitting them
at the time. He did not paint in raw realism.
He seized his characters firmly for the central
purpose of the play, stamped them in the
idea, and by slightly raising and softening the
object of study (as in the case of the ex-
Huguenot, Duke de Montausier,[1] for the
study of the Misanthrope, and, according to
St. Simon, the Abbé Roquette for Tartuffe),
generalized upon it so as to make it per-
manently human. Concede that it is natural
for human creatures to live in society, and
Alceste is an imperishable mark of one, though
he is drawn in light outline, without any
forcible human colouring. Our English school
has not clearly imagined society; and of the

---

[1] Tallemant des Réaux, in his rough portrait of the
Duke, shows the foundation of the character of Alceste.

mind hovering above congregated men and
women, it has imagined nothing. The critics
who praise it for its downrightness, and for
bringing the situations home to us, as they
admiringly say, cannot but disapprove of
Molière's comedy, which appeals to the indi-
vidual mind to perceive and participate in the
social. We have splendid tragedies, we have
the most beautiful of poetic plays, and we
have literary comedies passingly pleasant to
read, and occasionally to see acted. By
literary comedies, I mean comedies of classic
inspiration, drawn chiefly from Menander and
the Greek New Comedy through Terence;
or else comedies of the poet's personal conception, that have had no model in life, and
are humorous exaggerations, happy or otherwise. These are the comedies of Ben Jonson,
Massinger, and Fletcher. Massinger's Justice
Greedy we can all of us refer to a type, 'with
fat capon lined' that has been and will be;
and he would be comic, as Panurge is comic,
but only a Rabelais could set him moving

with real animation. Probably Justice Greedy would be comic to the audience of a country booth and to some of our friends. If we have lost our youthful relish for the presentation of characters put together to fit a type, we find it hard to put together the mechanism of a civil smile at his enumeration of his dishes. Something of the same is to be said of Boba-dil, swearing 'by the foot of Pharaoh'; with a reservation, for he is made to move faster, and to act. The comic of Jonson is a scholar's excogitation of the comic; that of Massinger a moralist's.

Shakespeare is a well-spring of characters which are saturated with the comic spirit; with more of what we will call blood-life than is to be found anywhere out of Shake-speare; and they are of this world, but they are of the world enlarged to our embrace by imagination, and by great poetic imagina-tion. They are, as it were—I put it to suit my present comparison—creatures of the woods and wilds, not in walled towns, not grouped and toned to pursue a comic exhibition of the narrower world of society. Jaques, Falstaff and his regiment, the varied troop of Clowns, Malvolio, Sir Hugh Evans and Fluellen — marvellous Welshmen ! — Benedict and Beatrice, Dogberry, and the rest, are subjects of a special study in the poetically comic.

His Comedy of incredible imbroglio belongs to the literary section. One may conceive that there was a natural resemblance between him and Menander, both in the scheme and style of his lighter plays. Had Shakespeare lived in a later and less emotional, less heroical period of our history, he might have turned to the painting of manners as well as humanity. Euripides would probably, in the time of Menander, when Athens was enslaved but prosperous, have lent his hand to the composition of romantic comedy. He certainly inspired that fine genius.

Politically it is accounted a misfortune for France that her nobles thronged to the Court

of Louis Quatorze. It was a boon to the
comic poet. He had that lively quicksilver
world of the animalcule passions, the huge
pretensions, the placid absurdities, under his
eyes in full activity; vociferous quacks and
snapping dupes, hypocrites, posturers, extra-
vagants, pedants, rose-pink ladies and mad
grammarians, sonnetteering marquises, high-
flying mistresses, plain-minded maids, inter-
threading as in a loom, noisy as at a fair.
A simply bourgeois circle will not furnish it,
for the middle class must have the brilliant,
flippant, independent upper for a spur and
a pattern; otherwise it is likely to be in-
wardly dull as well as outwardly correct.
Yet, though the King was benevolent toward
Molière, it is not to the French Court that
we are indebted for his unrivalled studies
of mankind in society. For the amusement
of the Court the ballets and farces were
written, which are dearer to the rabble
upper, as to the rabble lower, class than
intellectual comedy. The French bourgeoisie

of Paris were sufficiently quick-witted and enlightened by education to welcome great works like Le Tartuffe, Les Femmes Savantes, and Le Misanthrope, works that were perilous ventures on the popular intelligence, big vessels to launch on streams running to shallows. The Tartuffe hove into view as an enemy's vessel; it offended, not *Dieu mais les dévots*, as the Prince de Condé explained the cabal raised against it to the King.

The Femmes Savantes is a capital instance of the uses of comedy in teaching the world to understand what ails it. The farce of the *Précieuses* ridiculed and put a stop to the monstrous romantic jargon made popular by certain famous novels. The comedy of the Femmes Savantes exposed the later and less apparent but more finely comic absurdity of an excessive purism in grammar and diction, and the tendency to be idiotic in precision. The French had felt the burden of this new nonsense; but they had to see the comedy several times before they were consoled in their suffering by seeing the cause of it exposed.

The Misanthrope was yet more frigidly received. Molière thought it dead. 'I cannot improve on it, and assuredly never shall,' he said. It is one of the French titles to honour that this quintessential comedy of the opposition of Alceste and Célimène was ultimately understood and applauded. In all countries the middle class presents the public which, fighting the world, and with a good footing in the fight, knows the world best. It may be the most selfish, but that is a question leading us into sophistries. Cultivated men and women, who do not skim the cream of life, and are attached to the duties, yet escape the harsher blows, make acute and balanced observers. Molière is their poet.

Of this class in England, a large body, neither Puritan nor Bacchanalian, have a sentimental objection to face the study of

the actual world. They take up disdain of
it, when its truths appear humiliating: when
the facts are not immediately forced on
them, they take up the pride of incredulity.
They live in a hazy atmosphere that they
suppose an ideal one. Humorous writing
they will endure, perhaps approve, if it
mingles with pathos to shake and elevate
the feelings. They approve of Satire, because, like the beak of the vulture, it smells
of carrion, which they are not. But of
Comedy they have a shivering dread, for
Comedy enfolds them with the wretched host
of the world, huddles them with us all in
an ignoble assimilation, and cannot be used
by any exalted variety as a scourge and a
broom. Nay, to be an exalted variety is
to come under the calm curious eye of the
Comic spirit, and be probed for what you
are. Men are seen among them, and very
many cultivated women. You may distinguish them by a favourite phrase: 'Surely
we are not so bad!' and the remark: 'If

that is human nature, save us from it!' as
if it could be done: but in the peculiar
Paradise of the wilful people who will not
see, the exclamation assumes the saving
grace.

Yet should you ask them whether they
dislike sound sense, they vow they do not.
And question cultivated women whether it
pleases them to be shown moving on an
intellectual level with men, they will answer
that it does; numbers of them claim the
situation. Now, Comedy is the fountain of
sound sense; not the less perfectly sound
on account of the sparkle: and Comedy
lifts women to a station offering them free
play for their wit, as they usually show it,
when they have it, on the side of sound
sense. The higher the Comedy, the more
prominent the part they enjoy in it. Dorine
in the Tartuffe is common-sense incarnate,
though palpably a waiting-maid. Célimène
is undisputed mistress of the same attribute
in the Misanthrope; wiser as a woman than

Alceste as man. In Congreve's Way of the
World, Millamant overshadows Mirabel, the
sprightliest male figure of English comedy.

But those two ravishing women, so copious
and so choice of speech, who fence with men
and pass their guard, are heartless! Is it
not preferable to be the pretty idiot, the
passive beauty, the adorable bundle of ca-
prices, very feminine, very sympathetic, of
romantic and sentimental fiction? Our
women are taught to think so. The Agnès
of the École des Femmes should be a lesson
for men. The heroines of Comedy are like
women of the world, not necessarily heartless
from being clear-sighted: they seem so to
the sentimentally-reared only for the reason
that they use their wits, and are not wan-
dering vessels crying for a captain or a pilot.
Comedy is an exhibition of their battle with
men, and that of men with them: and as
the two, however divergent, both look on
one object, namely, Life, the gradual similarity of their impressions must bring them

to some resemblance. The Comic poet dares to show us men and women coming to this mutual likeness; he is for saying that when they draw together in social life their minds grow liker; just as the philosopher discerns the similarity of boy and girl, until the girl is marched away to the nursery. Philosopher and Comic poet are of a cousinship in the eye they cast on life: and they are equally unpopular with our wilful English of the hazy region and the ideal that is not to be disturbed.

Thus, for want of instruction in the Comic idea, we lose a large audience among our cultivated middle class that we should expect to support Comedy. The sentimentalist is as averse as the Puritan and as the Bacchanalian.

Our traditions are unfortunate. The public taste is with the idle laughers, and still inclines to follow them. It may be shown by an analysis of Wycherley's Plain Dealer, a coarse prose adaption of the Misanthrope, stuffed with lumps of realism in a vulgarized theme to hit the mark of English appetite, that we have in it the keynote of the Comedy of our stage. It is Molière travestied, with the hoof to his foot and hair on the pointed tip of his ear. And how difficult it is for writers to disentangle themselves from bad traditions is noticeable when we find Goldsmith, who had grave command of the Comic in narrative, producing an elegant farce for a Comedy; and Fielding, who was a master of the Comic both in narrative and in dialogue, not even approaching to the presentable in farce.

These bad traditions of Comedy affect us not only on the stage, but in our literature, and may be tracked into our social life. They are the ground of the heavy moralizings by which we are outwearied, about Life as a Comedy, and Comedy as a jade,[1] when popular

[1] See *Tom Jones* book VIII. chapter 1, for Fielding's opinion of our Comedy. But he puts it simply; not as an exercise in the quasi-philosophical bathetic.

writers, conscious of fatigue in creativeness,
desire to be cogent in a modish cynicism:
perversions of the idea of life, and of
the proper esteem for the society we have
wrested from brutishness, and would carry
higher. Stock images of this description are
accepted by the timid and the sensitive, as
well as by the saturnine, quite seriously; for
not many look abroad with their own eyes,
fewer still have the habit of thinking for
themselves. Life, we know too well, is not a
Comedy, but something strangely mixed;
nor is Comedy a vile mask. The corrupted
importation from France was noxious; a noble
entertainment spoilt to suit the wretched
taste of a villanous age; and the later imita-
tions of it, partly drained of its poison and
made decorous, became tiresome, notwithstanding their fun, in the perpetual recurring
of the same situations, owing to the absence
of original study and vigour of conception.
Scene v. Act 2 of the Misanthrope, owing, no
doubt, to the fact of our not producing matter

for original study, is repeated in succession
by Wycherley, Congreve, and Sheridan, and as
it is at second hand, we have it done cynically
— or such is the tone ; in the manner of 'below
stairs.' Comedy thus treated may be accepted
as a version of the ordinary worldly under-
standing of our social life; at least, in accord
with the current dicta concerning it. The
epigrams can be made ; but it is uninstruc-
tive, rather tending to do disservice. Comedy justly treated, as you find it in Molière,
whom we so clownishly mishandled, the
Comedy of Molière throws no infamous reflec-
tion upon life. It is deeply conceived, in the
first place, and therefore it cannot be impure.
Meditate on that statement. Never did man
wield so shrieking a scourge upon vice, but his
consummate self-mastery is not shaken while
administering it. Tartuffe and Harpagon, in
fact, are made each to whip himself and his
class, the false pietists, and the insanely covet-
ous. Molière has only set them in motion.
He strips Folly to the skin, displays the

imposture of the creature, and is content to offer her better clothing, with the lesson Chrysale reads to Philaminte and Bélise. He conceives purely, and he writes purely, in the simplest language, the simplest of French verse. The source of his wit is clear reason : it is a fountain of that soil; and it springs to vindicate reason, common-sense, rightness and justice; for no vain purpose ever. The wit is of such pervading spirit that it inspires a pun with meaning and interest.[1] His moral does not hang like a tail, or preach from one character incessantly cocking an eye at the audience, as in recent realistic French Plays : but is in the heart of his work, throbbing with every pulsation of an organic structure. If Life is likened to the comedy of Molière, there is no scandal in the comparison.

[1] *Femmes Savantes :*

BÉLISE : Veux-tu toute la vie offenser la grammaire ?

MARTINE : Qui parle d'offenser grand'mère ni grand-père ? '

The pun is delivered in all sincerity, from the mouth of a rustic.

Congreve's Way of the World is an excep-
tion to our other comedies, his own among
them, by virtue of the remarkable brilliancy
of the writing, and the figure of Millamant.
The comedy has no idea in it, beyond the
stale one, that so the world goes; and it con-
cludes with the jaded discovery of a document
at a convenient season for the descent of the
curtain.   A plot was an afterthought with
Congreve.   By the help of a wooden villain
(Maskwell) marked Gallows to the flattest eye,
he gets a sort of plot in The Double Dealer.[1]
His Way of the World might be called The
Conquest of a Town Coquette, and Millamant
is a perfect portrait of a coquette, both in her
resistance to Mirabel and the manner of her
surrender, and also in her tongue.   The wit
here is not so salient as in certain passages of

[1] Maskwell seems to have been carved on the model
of Iago, as by the hand of an enterprising urchin.   He
apostrophises his 'invention' repeatedly.   'Thanks,
my invention.'   He hits on an invention, to say:
'Was it my brain or Providence? no matter which.'
It is no matter which, but it was not his brain.

Love for Love, where Valentine feigns madness or retorts on his father, or Mrs. Frail rejoices in the harmlessness of wounds to a woman's virtue, if she ' keeps them from air.'   In The Way of the World, it appears less prepared in the smartness, and is more diffused in the more characteristic style of the speakers. Here, however, as elsewhere, his famous wit is like a bully-fencer, not ashamed to lay traps for its exhibition, transparently petulant for the train between certain ordinary words and the powder-magazine of the improprieties to be fired.   Contrast the wit of Congreve with Molière's.   That of the first is a Toledo blade, sharp, and wonderfully supple for steel; cast for duelling, restless in the scabbard, being so pretty when out of it.   To shine, it must have an adversary.   Molière's wit is like a running brook, with innumerable fresh lights on it at every turn of the wood through which its business is to find a way.   It does not run in search of obstructions, to be noisy over them; but when dead leaves and viler sub-

stances are heaped along the course, its natural
song is heightened. Without effort, and with
no dazzling flashes of achievement, it is full of
healing, the wit of good breeding, the wit of
wisdom.

'Genuine humour and true wit,' says
Landor,[1] 'require a sound and capacious mind,
which is always a grave one. Rabelais and La
Fontaine are recorded by their countrymen to
have been *rêveurs*. Few men have been graver
than Pascal. Few men have been wittier.'

To apply the citation of so great a brain as
Pascal's to our countryman would be unfair.
Congreve had a certain soundness of mind; of
capacity, in the sense intended by Landor, he
had little. Judging him by his wit, he performed some happy thrusts, and taking it for
genuine, it is a surface wit, neither rising from
a depth nor flowing from a spring.

'On voit qu'il se travaille à dire de bons mots.'

He drives the poor hack word, 'fool,' as

[1] *Imaginary Conversations :* Alfieri and the Jew
Salomon.

cruelly to the market for wit as any of his competitors.   Here is an example, that has been held up for eulogy :

WITWOUD : He has brought me a letter from the fool my brother, etc. etc.

MIRABEL :   A fool, and your brother, Wit-woud ?

WITWOUD :   Ay, ay, my half-brother.   My half-brother he is ;   no nearer, upon my honour.

MIRABEL :   Then 'tis possible he may be but half a fool.

By evident preparation.   This is a sort of wit one remembers to have heard at school, of a brilliant outsider ;   perhaps to have been guilty of oneself, a trifle later.   It was, no doubt, a blaze of intellectual fireworks to the bumpkin squire, who came to London to go to the theatre and learn manners.

Where Congreve excels all his English rivals is in his literary force, and a succinctness of style peculiar to him.   He had correct judgment, a correct ear, readiness of illustra-

tion within a narrow range, in snapshots of the
obvious at the obvious, and copious language.
He hits the mean of a fine style and a natural
in dialogue. He is at once precise and
voluble. If you have ever thought upon style
you will acknowledge it to be a signal accom-
plishment. In this he is a classic, and is
worthy of treading a measure with Molière.
The Way of the World may be read out cur-
rently at a first glance, so sure are the accents
of the emphatic meaning to strike the eye,
perforce of the crispness and cunning polish of
the sentences. You have not to look over
them before you confide yourself to him; he
will carry you safe. Sheridan imitated, but
was far from surpassing him. The flow of
boudoir Billingsgate in Lady Wishfort is
unmatched for the vigour and pointedness
of the tongue. It spins along with a final
ring, like the voice of Nature in a fury, and
is, indeed, racy eloquence of the elevated
fishwife.

Millamant is an admirable, almost a lovable

heroine. It is a piece of genius in a writer to make a woman's manner of speech portray her. You feel sensible of her presence in every line of her speaking. The stipulations with her lover in view of marriage, her fine lady's delicacy, and fine lady's easy evasions of indelicacy, coquettish airs, and playing with irresolution, which in a common maid would be bashfulness, until she submits to 'dwindle into a wife,' as she says, form a picture that lives in the frame, and is in harmony with Mirabel's description of her :

'Here she comes, i' faith, full sail, with her fan spread, and her streamers out, and a shoal of fools for tenders.'

And, after an interview :

'Think of you! To think of a whirlwind, though 'twere in a whirlwind, were a case of more steady contemplation, a very tranquillity of mind and mansion.'

There is a picturesqueness, as of Millamant and no other, in her voice, when she is encouraged to take Mirabel by Mrs. Fainall, who is 'sure she has a mind to him':

MILLAMANT: Are you? I think I have — and the horrid man looks as if he thought so too, etc. etc.

One hears the tones, and sees the sketch and colour of the whole scene in reading it.

Célimène is behind Millamant in vividness. An air of bewitching whimsicality hovers over the graces of this Comic heroine, like the lively conversational play of a beautiful mouth.

But in wit she is no rival of Célimène. What she utters adds to her personal witchery, and is not further memorable. She is a flashing portrait, and a type of the superior ladies who do not think, not of those who do. In representing a class, therefore, it is a lower class, in the proportion that one of Gainsborough's full-length aristocratic women is below the permanent impressiveness of a fair Venetian head.

Millamant side by side with Célimène is an example of how far the realistic painting of a character can be carried to win our favour; and of where it falls short. Célimène is a woman's mind in movement, armed with an ungovernable wit; with perspicacious clear eyes for the world, and a very distinct knowledge that she belongs to the world, and is most at home in it. She is attracted to Alceste by her esteem for his honesty; she cannot avoid seeing where the good sense of the man is diseased.

Rousseau, in his letter to D'Alembert on the subject of the Misanthrope, discusses the character of Alceste, as though Molière had put him forth for an absolute example of misanthropy; whereas Alceste is only a misanthrope of the circle he finds himself placed in: he has a touching faith in the virtue residing in the country, and a critical love of sweet simpleness. Nor is he the principal person of the comedy to which he gives a name. He is only passively comic.

Célimène is the active spirit. While he is
denouncing and railing, the trial is imposed
upon her to make the best of him, and
control herself, as much as a witty woman,
eagerly courted, can do. By appreciating
him she practically confesses her faultiness,
and she is better disposed to meet him half
way than he is to bend an inch: only she
is *une âme de vingt ans*, the world is pleasant, and if the gilded flies of the Court are
silly, uncompromising fanatics have their
ridiculous features as well. Can she abandon the life they make agreeable to her,
for a man who will not be guided by the
common sense of his class; and who insists
on plunging into one extreme — equal to
suicide in her eyes — to avoid another? That
is the comic question of the Misanthrope.
Why will he not continue to mix with the
world smoothly, appeased by the flattery of
her secret and really sincere preference of
him, and taking his revenge in satire of it,
as she does from her own not very lofty

standard, and will by and by do from his more exalted one?

Célimène is worldliness: Alceste is unworldliness. It does not quite imply unselfishness; and that is perceived by her shrewd head. Still he is a very uncommon figure in her circle, and she esteems him, *l'homme aux rubans verts*, 'who sometimes diverts but more often horribly vexes her,' as she can say of him when her satirical tongue is on the run. Unhappily the soul of truth in him, which wins her esteem, refuses to be tamed, or silent, or unsuspicious, and is the perpetual obstacle to their good accord. He is that melancholy person, the critic of everybody save himself; intensely sensitive to the faults of others, wounded by them; in love with his own indubitable honesty, and with his ideal of the simpler form of life befitting it: qualities which constitute the satirist. He is a Jean Jacques of the Court. His proposal to Célimène when he pardons her, that she should follow him in flying humankind, and his frenzy of detestation of her at her refusal, are thoroughly in the mood of Jean Jacques. He is an impracticable creature of a priceless virtue; but Célimène may feel that to fly with him to the desert: that is, from the Court to the country:

'Où d'être homme d'honneur on ait la liberté,'

she is likely to find herself the companion of a starving satirist, like that poor princess who ran away with the waiting-man, and when both were hungry in the forest, was ordered to give him flesh. She is a *fieffée* coquette, rejoicing in her wit and her attractions, and distinguished by her inclination for Alceste in the midst of her many other lovers; only she finds it hard to cut them off — what woman with a train does not? — and when the exposure of her naughty wit has laid her under their rebuke, she will do the utmost she can: she will give her hand to honesty, but she cannot quite abandon worldliness. She would be unwise if she did.

The fable is thin. Our pungent contrivers of plots would see no indication of life in the outlines. The life of the comedy is in the idea. As with the singing of the sky-lark out of sight, you must love the bird to be attentive to the song, so in this highest flight of the Comic Muse, you must love pure Comedy warmly to understand the Misanthrope : you must be receptive of the idea of Comedy. And to love Comedy you must know the real world, and know men and women well enough not to expect too much of them, though you may still hope for good.

Menander wrote a comedy called Misogynes, said to have been the most celebrated of his works. This misogynist is a married man, according to the fragment surviving, and is a hater of women through hatred of his wife. He generalizes upon them from the example of this lamentable adjunct of his fortunes, and seems to have got the worst of it in the contest with her, which is like the issue in reality, in the polite world. He seems also to have deserved it, which may be as true to the copy. But we are unable to say whether the wife was a good voice of her sex: or how far Menander in this instance raised the idea of woman from the mire it was plunged into by the comic poets, or rather satiric dramatists, of the middle period of Greek Comedy preceding him and the New Comedy, who devoted their wit chiefly to the abuse, and for a diversity, to the eulogy of extra-mural ladies of conspicuous fame. Menander idealized them without purposely elevating. He satirised a certain Thais, and his Thais of the Eunuchus of Terence is neither professionally attractive nor repulsive; his picture of the two Andrians, Chrysis and her sister, is nowhere to be matched for tenderness. But the condition of honest women in his day did not permit of the freedom of action and fencing dialectic of a Célimène, and consequently it is below our mark of pure Comedy.

Sainte-Beuve conjures up the ghost of Menander, saying : For the love of me love Terence. It is through love of Terence that moderns are able to love Menander; and what is preserved of Terence has not apparently given us the best of the friend of Epicurus. Μισούμενος the lover taken in horror, and Περικειρομένη the damsel shorn of her locks, have a promising sound for scenes of jealousy and a too masterful display of lordly authority, leading to regrets, of the kind known to intemperate men who imagined they were fighting with the weaker, as the fragments indicate.

Of the six comedies of Terence, four are derived from Menander; two, the Hecyra and the Phormio, from Apollodorus. These two are inferior in comic action and the peculiar sweetness of Menander to the Andria, the Adelphi, the Heautontimorumenus, and the Eunuchus: but Phormio is a more dashing and amusing convivial parasite than the Gnatho of the last-named comedy. There were numerous rivals of whom we know next to nothing — except by the quotations of Athenæus and Plutarch, and the Greek grammarians who cited them to support a dictum — in this as in the preceding periods of comedy in Athens, for Menander's plays are counted by many scores, and they were crowned by the prize only eight times. The favourite poet with critics, in Greece as in Rome, was Menander; and if some of his rivals here and there surpassed him in comic force, and outstripped him in competition by an appositeness to the occasion that had previously in the same way deprived the genius of Aristophanes of its due reward in Clouds and Birds, his position as chief of the comic poets of his age was unchallenged. Plutarch very unnecessarily drags Aristophanes into a comparison with him, to the confusion of the older poet. Their aims, the matter they dealt in, and the times, were quite dissimilar. But it is no wonder that Plutarch, writing when Athenian beauty of style was the delight of his patrons, should rank Menander at the highest. In what

degree of faithfulness Terence copied Menander,
whether, as he states of the passage in the
Adelphi taken from Diphilus, *verbum de verbo*
in the lovelier scenes — the description of the
last words of the dying Andrian, and of her
funeral, for instance — remains conjectural. For
us Terence shares with his master the praise
of an amenity that is like Elysian speech,
equable and ever gracious; like the face of
the Andrian's young sister:

'Adeo modesto, adeo venusto, ut nihil supra.'

The celebrated 'flens quam familiariter,' of
which the closest rendering grounds hopelessly
on harsh prose, to express the sorrowful con-
fidingness of a young girl who has lost her
sister and dearest friend, and has but her lover
left to her; 'she turned and flung herself on
his bosom, weeping as though at home there':
this our instinct tells us must be Greek,
though hardly finer in Greek.   Certain lines
of Terence, compared with the original fragments, show that he embellished them; but his

taste was too exquisite for him to do other than devote his genius to the honest translation of such pieces as the above. Menander, then; with him, through the affinity of sympathy, Terence; and Shakespeare and Molière have this beautiful translucency of language: and the study of the comic poets might be recommended, if for that only.

A singular ill fate befell the writings of Menander. What we have of him in Terence was chosen probably to please the cultivated Romans;[1] and is a romantic play with a comic intrigue, obtained in two instances, the Andria and the Eunuchus, by rolling a couple of his originals into one. The titles of certain of the lost plays indicate the comic illumining character; a Self-pitier, a Self-chastiser, an Ill-tempered man, a Superstitious, an Incredulous, etc., point to suggestive domestic themes.

[1] Terence did not please the rough old conservative Romans; they liked Plautus better, and the recurring mention of the *vetus poeta* in his prologues, who plagued him with the crusty critical view of his productions, has in the end a comic effect on the reader.

Terence forwarded manuscript translations
from Greece, that suffered shipwreck ; he, who
could have restored the treasure, died on the
way home. The zealots of Byzantium com-
pleted the work of destruction. So we have
the four comedies of Terence, numbering six
of Menander, with a few sketches of plots —
one of them, the Thesaurus, introduces a miser,
whom we should have liked to contrast with
Harpagon — and a multitude of small fragments of a sententious cast, fitted for quota-
tion. Enough remains to make his greatness
felt.

Without undervaluing other writers of
Comedy, I think it may be said that Menander
and Molière stand alone specially as comic
poets of the feelings and the idea. In each of
them there is a conception of the Comic that
refines even to pain, as in the Menedemus of
the Heautontimorumenus, and in the Misanthrope. Menander and Molière have given
the principal types to Comedy hitherto. The
Micio and Demea of the Adelphi, with their

opposing views of the proper management of youth, are still alive; the Sganarelles and Arnolphes of the École des Maris and the École des Femmes, are not all buried. Tartuffe is the father of the hypocrites; Orgon of the dupes; Thraso, of the braggadocios; Alceste of the 'Manlys'; Davus and Syrus of the intriguing valets, the Scapins and Figaros. Ladies that soar in the realms of Rose-Pink, whose language wears the nodding plumes of intellectual conceit, are traceable to Philaminte and Bélise of the Femmes Savantes; and the mordant witty women have the tongue of Célimène. The reason is, that these two poets idealized upon life: the foundation of their types is real and in the quick, but they painted with spiritual strength, which is the solid in Art.

The idealistic conception of Comedy gives breadth and opportunities of daring to Comic genius, and helps to solve the difficulties it creates. How, for example, shall an audience be assured that an evident and monstrous dupe

is actually deceived without being an absolute
fool ? In Le Tartuffe the note of high Comedy
strikes when Orgon on his return home hears
of his idol's excellent appetite. ' *Le pauvre
homme !* ' he exclaims. He is told that the
wife of his bosom has been unwell. ' *Et Tartuffe ?* ' he asks, impatient to hear him spoken
of, his mind suffused with the thought of
Tartuffe, crazy with tenderness, and again he
croons, ' *Le pauvre homme !* ' It is the mother's
cry of pitying delight at a nurse's recital of the
feats in young animal gluttony of her cherished
infant. After this masterstroke of the Comic,
you not only put faith in Orgon's roseate pre-
possession, you share it with him by comic
sympathy, and can listen with no more than
a tremble of the laughing muscles to the
instance he gives of the sublime humanity of
Tartuffe :

> ' Un rien presque suffit pour le scandaliser,
> Jusque-là, qu'il se vint l'autre jour accuser
> D'avoir pris une puce en faisant sa prière,
> Et de l'avoir tuée avec trop de colère.'

And to have killed it too wrathfully! Translating <u>Molière</u> is like humming an air one has heard performed by an accomplished violinist of the pure tones without flourish.

Orgon, awakening to find another dupe in Madame Pernelle, incredulous of the revelations which have at last opened his own besotted eyes, is a scene of the double Comic, vivified by the spell previously cast on the mind. There we feel the power of the poet's creation; and in the sharp light of that sudden turn the humanity is livelier than any realistic work can make it.

Italian Comedy gives many hints for a Tartuffe; but they may be found in Boccaccio, as well as in Machiavelli's Mandragola. The Frate Timoteo of this piece is only a very oily friar, compliantly assisting an intrigue with ecclesiastical sophisms (to use the mildest word) for payment. Frate Timoteo has a fine Italian priestly pose.

DONNA: *Credete voi, che'l Turco passi questo anno in Italia?*

4

F. Tim. : *Se voi non fate orazione, sì.*

Priestly arrogance and unctuousness, and trickeries and casuistries, cannot be painted without our discovering a likeness in the long Italian gallery. Goldoni sketched the Venetian manners of the decadence of the Republic with a French pencil, and was an Italian scribe in style.

The Spanish stage is richer in such Comedies as that which furnished the idea of the Menteur to Corneille. But you must force yourself to believe that this liar is not forcing his vein when he piles lie upon lie. There is no preceding touch to win the mind to credulity. Spanish Comedy is generally in sharp outline, as of skeletons; in quick movement, as of marionnettes. The Comedy might be performed by a troop of the *corps de ballet;* and in the recollection of the reading it resolves to an animated shuffle of feet. It is, in fact, something other than the true idea of Comedy. Where the sexes are separated, men and women grow, as the Portuguese call it, *affaima-*

dos of one another, famine-stricken; and all
the tragic elements are on the stage. Don
Juan is a comic character that sends souls
flying: nor does the humour of the breaking
of a dozen women's hearts conciliate the Comic
Muse with the drawing of blood.

German attempts at Comedy remind one
vividly of Heine's image of his country in the
dancing of Atta Troll. Lessing tried his
hand at it, with a sobering effect upon readers.
The intention to produce the reverse effect is
just visible, and therein, like the portly graces
of the poor old Pyrenean Bear poising and
twirling on his right hind-leg and his left,
consists the fun. Jean Paul Richter gives the
best edition of the German Comic in the contrast of Siebenkäs with his Lenette. A light of
the Comic is in Goethe; enough to complete
the splendid figure of the man, but no more.

The German literary laugh, like the timed
awakenings of their Barbarossa in the hollows
of the Untersberg, is infrequent, and rather
monstrous — never a laugh of men and women

in concert. It comes of unrefined abstract
fancy, grotesque or grim, or gross, like the
peculiar humours of their little earthmen.
Spiritual laughter they have not yet attained
to : sentimentalism waylays them in the flight.
Here and there a Volkslied or Märchen shows
a national aptitude for stout animal laughter;
and we see that the literature is built on it,
which is hopeful so far ; but to enjoy it, to
enter into the philosophy of the Broad Grin,
that seems to hesitate between the skull and the
embryo, and reaches its perfection in breadth
from the pulling of two square fingers at the
corners of the mouth, one must have aid of
' the good Rhine wine,' and be of German
blood unmixed besides.   This treble-Dutch
lumbersomeness of the Comic spirit is of itself exclusive of the idea of Comedy, and the
poor voice allowed to women in German
domestic life will account for the absence of
comic dialogues reflecting upon life in that
land.   I shall speak of it again in the second
section of this lecture.

Eastward you have total silence of Comedy among a people intensely susceptible to laughter, as the *Arabian Nights* will testify. Where the veil is over women's faces, you cannot have society, without which the senses are barbarous and the Comic Spirit is driven to the gutters of grossness to slake its thirst. Arabs in this respect are worse than Italians — much worse than Germans ; just in the degree that their system of treating women is worse.

M. Saint-Marc Girardin, the excellent French essayist and master of critical style, tells of a conversation he had once with an Arab gentleman on the topic of the different management of these difficult creatures in Orient and in Occident: and the Arab spoke in praise of many good results of the greater freedom enjoyed by Western ladies, and the charm of conversing with them. He was questioned why his countrymen took no measures to grant them something of that kind of liberty. He jumped out of his individuality in a twinkling, and entered into the sentiments of his race, replying, from the pinnacle of a splendid conceit, with affected humility of manner: ' *You* can look on them without perturbation — but *we!* ' . . . And after this profoundly comic interjection, he added, in deep tones, ' The very face of a woman ! ' Our representative of temperate notions demurely consented that the Arab's pride of inflammability should insist on the prudery of the veil as the civilizing medium of his race.

There has been fun in Bagdad. But there never will be civilization where Comedy is not possible; and that comes of some degree of social equality of the sexes. I am not quoting the Arab to exhort and disturb the somnolent East; rather for cultivated women to recognize that the Comic Muse is one of their best friends. They are blind to their interests in swelling the ranks of the sentimentalists. Let them look with their clearest vision abroad and at home. They will see that where they have no social freedom, Comedy is absent: where they are household drudges, the form of Comedy is primitive: where they are tolerably independent, but uncultivated, exciting melodrama takes its place and a sentimental version of them. Yet the Comic will out, as they would know if they listened to some of the private conversations of men whose minds are undirected by the Comic Muse: as the sentimental man, to his astonishment, would know likewise, if he in similar fashion could receive a lesson. But where women are on the road to an equal footing with men, in attainments and in liberty — in what they have won for themselves, and what has been granted them by a fair civilization — there, and only waiting to be transplanted from life to the stage, or the novel, or the poem, pure Comedy flourishes, and is, as it would help them to be, the sweetest of diversions, the wisest of delightful companions.

Now, to look about us in the present time, I think it will be acknowledged that in neglecting the cultivation of the Comic idea, we are losing the aid of a powerful auxiliar. You see Folly perpetually sliding into new shapes in a society possessed of wealth and leisure, with many whims, many strange ailments and strange doctors. Plenty of common-sense is in the world to thrust her back when she pretends to empire. But the first-born of common-sense, the vigilant Comic, which is the genius of thoughtful laughter, which would readily extinguish her at the outset, is not serving as a public advocate.

You will have noticed the disposition of common-sense, under pressure of some pertinacious piece of light-headedness, to grow impatient and angry. That is a sign of the absence, or at least of the dormancy, of the Comic idea. For Folly is the natural prey of the Comic, known to it in all her transformations, in every disguise; and it is with the springing delight of hawk over heron, hound after fox, that it gives her chase, never fretting, never tiring, sure of having her, allowing her no rest.

Contempt is a sentiment that cannot be entertained by comic intelligence. What is it but an excuse to be idly minded, or personally lofty, or comfortably narrow, not perfectly humane? If we do not feign when we say that we despise Folly, we shut the brain. There is a disdainful attitude in the presence of Folly, partaking of the foolishness to Comic perception: and anger is not much less foolish than disdain. The struggle we have to conduct is essence against essence. Let no one doubt of the sequel when this emanation of what is firmest in us is launched to strike down the daughter of Unreason and Sentimentalism: such being Folly's parentage, when it is respectable.

Our modern system of combating her is too long defensive, and carried on too ploddingly with concrete engines of war in the attack. She has time to get behind entrenchments. She is ready to stand a siege, before the heavily armed man of science and the writer of the leading article or elaborate essay have

primed their big guns. It should be remem-
bered that she has charms for the multitude;
and an English multitude seeing her make a
gallant fight of it will be half in love with her,
certainly willing to lend her a cheer. Benevolent subscriptions assist her to hire her own
man of science, her own organ in the Press.
If ultimately she is cast out and overthrown,
she can stretch a finger at gaps in our ranks.
She can say that she commanded an army and
seduced men, whom we thought sober men and
safe, to act as her lieutenants. We learn
rather gloomily, after she has flashed her
lantern, that we have in our midst able men
and men with minds for whom there is no
pole star in intellectual navigation. Comedy,
or the Comic element, is the specific for the
poison of delusion while Folly is passing
from the state of vapour to substantial form.

O for a breath of Aristophanes, Rabelais,
Voltaire, Cervantes, Fielding, Molière! These
are spirits that, if you know them well, will
come when you do call. You will find the.

very invocation of them act on you like a renovating air — the South-west coming off the sea, or a cry in the Alps.

No one would presume to say that we are deficient in jokers. They abound, and the organisation directing their machinery to shoot them in the wake of the leading article and the popular sentiment is good.

But the Comic differs from them in addressing the wits for laughter; and the sluggish wits want some training to respond to it, whether in public life or private, and particularly when the feelings are excited.

The sense of the Comic is much blunted by habits of punning and of using humouristic phrase: the trick of employing Johnsonian polysyllables to treat of the infinitely little. And it really may be humorous, of a kind, yet it will miss the point by going too much round about it.

A certain French Duke Pasquier died, some years back, at a very advanced age. He had been the venerable Duke Pasquier in his later

years up to the period of his death. There
was a report of Duke Pasquier that he was a
man of profound egoism.   Hence an argument
arose, and was warmly sustained, upon the
excessive selfishness of those who, in a world
of troubles, and calls to action, and innumerable duties, husband their strength for the
sake of living on. Can it be possible, the
argument ran, for a truly generous heart to
continue beating up to the age of a hundred?
Duke Pasquier was not without his defenders,
who likened him to the oak of the forest — a
venerable comparison.

The argument was conducted on both sides
with spirit and earnestness, lightened here and
there by frisky touches of the polysyllabic
playful, reminding one of the serious pursuit
of their fun by truant boys, that are assured
they are out of the eye of their master, and
now and then indulge in an imitation of him.
And well might it be supposed that the Comic
idea was asleep, not overlooking them! It
resolved at last to this, that either Duke Pas-

quier was a scandal on our humanity in cling-
ing to life so long, or that he honoured it by
so sturdy a resistance to the enemy. As one
who has entangled himself in a labyrinth is
glad to get out again at the entrance, the
argument ran about to conclude with its commencement.

Now, imagine a master of the Comic treating this theme, and particularly the argument
on it. Imagine an Aristophanic comedy of
The Centenarian, with choric praises of heroical
early death, and the same of a stubborn
vitality, and the poet laughing at the chorus;
and the grand question for contention in
dialogue, as to the exact age when a man
should die, to the identical minute, that he
may preserve the respect of his fellows, followed by a systematic attempt to make an
accurate measurement in parallel lines, with a
tough rope-yarn by one party, and a string of
yawns by the other, of the veteran's power of
enduring life, and our capacity for enduring
him, with tremendous pulling on both sides.

Would not the Comic view of the discussion illumine it and the disputants like very lightning? There are questions, as well as persons, that only the Comic can fitly touch.

Aristophanes would probably have crowned the ancient tree, with the consolatory observation to the haggard line of long-expectant heirs of the Centenarian, that they live to see the blessedness of coming of a strong stock. The shafts of his ridicule would mainly have been aimed at the disputants. For the sole ground of the argument was the old man's character, and sophists are not needed to demonstrate that we can very soon have too much of a bad thing. A Centenarian does not necessarily provoke the Comic idea, nor does the corpse of a duke. It is not provoked in the order of nature, until we draw its penetrating attentiveness to some circumstance with which we have been mixing our private interests, or our speculative obfuscation. Dulness, insensible to the Comic, has the privilege of arousing it; and the laying of a dull finger on matters of human life is the surest method of establishing electrical communications with a battery of laughter — where the Comic idea is prevalent.

But if the Comic idea prevailed with us, and we had an Aristophanes to barb and wing it, we should be breathing air of Athens. Prosers now pouring forth on us like public fountains would be cut short in the street and left blinking, dumb as pillar-posts, with letters thrust into their mouths. We should throw off incubus, our dreadful familiar — by some called boredom — whom it is our present humiliation to be just alive enough to loathe, never quick enough to foil. There would be a bright and positive, clear Hellenic perception of facts. The vapours of Unreason and Sentimentalism would be blown away before they were productive. Where would Pessimist and Optimist be? They would in any case have a diminished audience. Yet possibly the change of despots, from good-natured old obtuseness to keen-edged intelligence, which

is by nature ˉmerciless, would be more than we
could bear. The rupture of the link between
dull people, consisting in the fraternal agree-
ment that something is too clever for them,
and a shot beyond them, is not to be thought
of lightly; for, slender though the link may
seem, it is equivalent to a cement forming a
concrete of dense cohesion, very desirable in
the estimation of the statesman.

A political Aristophanes, taking advantage
of his lyrical Bacchic licence, was found too
much for political Athens. I would not ask
to have him revived, but that the sharp light
of such a spirit as his might be with us to
strike now and then on public affairs, public
themes, to make them spin along more
briskly.

He hated with the politician's fervour the
sophist who corrupted simplicity of thought,
the poet who destroyed purity of style, the
demagogue, ' the saw-toothed monster,' who,
as he conceived, chicaned the mob, and he
held his own against them by strength of

laughter, until fines, the curtailing of his Comic licence in the chorus, and ultimately the ruin of Athens, which could no longer support the expense of the chorus, threw him altogether on dialogue, and brought him under the law. After the catastrophe, the poet, who had ever been gazing back at the men of Marathon and Salamis, must have felt that he had foreseen it; and that he was wise when he pleaded for peace, and derided military coxcombry, and the captious old creature Demus, we can admit. He had the Comic poet's gift of common-sense — which does not always include political intelligence; yet his political tendency raised him above the Old Comedy turn for uproarious farce. He abused Socrates, but Xenophon, the disciple of Socrates, by his trained rhetoric saved the Ten Thousand. Aristophanes might say that if his warnings had been followed there would have been no such thing as a mercenary Greek expedition under Cyrus. Athens, however, was on a landslip, falling; none could arrest it. To gaze back, to uphold the old times, was a most natural conservatism, and fruitless. The aloe had bloomed. Whether right or wrong in his politics and his criticisms, and bearing in mind the instruments he played on and the audience he had to win, there is an idea in his comedies : it is the Idea of Good Citizenship.

He is not likely to be revived. He stands, like Shakespeare, an unapproachable. Swift says of him, with a loving chuckle :

> ' But as for Comic Aristophanes,
> The dog too witty and too prófane is.'

Aristophanes was ' prófane,' under satiric direction, unlike his rivals Cratinus, Phrynichus, Ameipsias, Eupolis, and others, if we are to believe him, who in their extraordinary Donnybrook Fair of the day of Comedy, thumped one another and everybody else with absolute heartiness, as he did, but aimed at small game, and dragged forth particular women, which he did not. He is an aggregate of many men, all of a certain greatness. We may build up a conception of his powers if we mount Rabelais upon Hudibras, lift him with the songfulness of Shelley, give him a vein of Heinrich Heine, and cover him with the mantle of the Anti-Jacobin, adding (that there may be some Irish in him) a dash of Grattan, before he is in motion.

But such efforts at conceiving one great one by incorporation of minors are vain, and cry for excuse. Supposing Wilkes for leading man in a country constantly plunging into war under some plumed Lamachus, with enemies periodically firing the land up to the gates of London, and a Samuel Foote, of prodigious genius, attacking him with ridicule, I think it gives a notion of the conflict engaged in by Aristophanes. This laughing bald-pate, as he calls himself, was a Titanic pamphleteer, using laughter for his political weapon; a laughter without scruple, the laughter of Hercules. He was primed with wit, as with the garlic he speaks of giving to

the game-cocks, to make them fight the better.
And he was a lyric poet of aerial delicacy,
with the homely song of a jolly national poet,
and a poet of such feeling that the comic
mask is at times no broader than a cloth on a
face to show the serious features of our common likeness. He is not to be revived; but if
his method were studied, some of the fire in
him would come to us, and we might be
revived.

Taking them generally, the English public
are most in sympathy with this primitive
Aristophanic comedy, wherein the comic is
capped by the grotesque, irony tips the wit,
and satire is a naked sword. They have the
basis of the Comic in them: an esteem for
common-sense. They cordially dislike the
reverse of it. They have a rich laugh, though
it is not the *gros rire* of the Gaul tossing *gros
sel*, nor the polished Frenchman's mentally
digestive laugh. And if they have now, like
a monarch with a troop of dwarfs, too many
jesters kicking the dictionary about, to let

them reflect that they are dull, occasionally, like the pensive monarch surprising himself with an idea of an idea of his own, they look so. And they are given to looking in the glass. They must see that something ails them. How much even the better order of them will endure, without a thought of the defensive, when the person afflicting them is protected from satire, we read in Memoirs of a Preceding Age, where the vulgarly tyrannous hostess of a great house of reception shuffled the guests and played them like a pack of cards, with her exact estimate of the strength of each one printed on them: and still this house continued to be the most popular in England; nor did the lady ever appear in print or on the boards as the comic type that she was.

It has been suggested that they have not yet spiritually comprehended the signification of living in society; for who are cheerfuller, brisker of wit, in the fields, and as explorers, colonizers, backwoodsmen? They are happy in rough exercise, and also in complete repose. The intermediate condition, when they are called upon to talk to one another, upon other than affairs of business or their hobbies, reveals them wearing a curious look of vacancy, as it were the socket of an eye wanting. The Comic is perpetually springing up in social life, and it oppresses them from not being perceived.

Thus, at a dinner-party, one of the guests, who happens to have enrolled himself in a Burial Company, politely entreats the others to inscribe their names as shareholders, expatiating on the advantages accruing to them in the event of their very possible speedy death, the salubrity of the site, the aptitude of the soil for a quick consumption of their remains, etc. ; and they drink sadness from the incongruous man, and conceive indigestion, not seeing him in a sharply defined light, that would bid them taste the comic of him. Or it is mentioned that a newly elected member of our Parliament celebrates his arrival at eminence by the publication of a book on cab-fares, dedicated to a beloved female relative deceased, and the comment on it is the word 'Indeed.' But, merely for a contrast, turn to a not uncommon scene of yesterday in the hunting-field, where a brilliant young rider, having broken his collar-bone, trots away very soon after, against medical interdict, half put together in splinters, to the most distant meet of his neighbourhood, sure of escaping his doctor, who is the first person he encounters. 'I came here purposely to avoid you,' says the patient. 'I came here purposely to take care of you,' says the doctor. Off they go, and come to a swollen brook. The patient clears it handsomely: the doctor tumbles in. All the field are alive with the heartiest relish of every incident and every cross-light on it; and dull would the man have been thought who had not his word to say about it when riding home.

In our prose literature we have had delight-ful Comic writers. Besides Fielding and Gold-

smith, there is Miss Austen, whose Emma and
Mr. Elton might walk straight into a comedy,
were the plot arranged for them. Galt's
neglected novels have some characters and
strokes of shrewd comedy. In our poetic
literature the comic is delicate and graceful
above the touch of Italian and French. Generally, however, the English elect excel in satire,
and they are noble humourists. The national
disposition is for hard-hitting, with a moral
purpose to sanction it ; or for a rosy, sometimes a larmoyant, geniality, not unmanly in
its verging upon tenderness, and with a singular attraction for thick-headedness, to decorate
it with asses' ears and the most beautiful
sylvan haloes. But the Comic is a different
spirit.

You may estimate your capacity for Comic
perception by being able to detect the ridicule
of them you love, without loving them less :
and more by being able to see yourself some-
what ridiculous in dear eyes, and accepting
the correction their image of you proposes.

Each one of an affectionate couple may be willing, as we say, to die for the other, yet, unwilling to utter the agreeable word at the right moment ; but if the wits were sufficiently quick for them to perceive that they are in a comic situation, as affectionate couples must be when they quarrel, they would not wait for the moon or the almanac, or a Dorine, to bring back the flood-tide of tender feelings, that they should join hands and lips.

If you detect the ridicule, and your kindliness is chilled by it, you are slipping into the grasp of Satire.

If instead of falling foul of the ridiculous person with a satiric rod, to make him writhe and shriek aloud, you prefer to sting him under a semi-caress, by which he shall in his anguish be rendered dubious whether indeed anything has hurt him, you are an engine of Irony.

If you laugh all round him, tumble him, roll him about, deal him a smack, and drop a tear on him, own his likeness to you and yours

to your neighbour, spare him as little as
you shun, pity him as much as you expose,
it is a spirit of Humour that is moving
you.

The Comic, which is the perceptive, is the
governing spirit, awakening and giving aim to
these powers of laughter, but it is not to be
confounded with them: it enfolds a thinner
form of them, differing from satire, in not
sharply driving into the quivering sensibilities,
and from humour, in not comforting them and
tucking them up, or indicating a broader
than the range of this bustling world to
them.

Fielding's Jonathan Wild presents a case
of this peculiar distinction, when that man of
eminent greatness remarks upon the unfairness
of a trial in which the condemnation has been
brought about by twelve men of the opposite
party; for it is not satiric, it is not humorous;
yet it is immensely comic to hear a guilty
villain protesting that his own 'party' should
have a voice in the Law.   It opens an avenue

into villains' ratiocination.[1] And the Comic is not cancelled though we should suppose Jonathan to be giving play to his humour. I may have dreamed this or had it suggested to me, for on referring to *Jonathan Wild*, I do not find it.

Apply the case to the man of deep wit, who is ever certain of his condemnation by the opposite party, and then it ceases to be comic, and will be satiric.

The look of Fielding upon Richardson is essentially comic. His method of correcting the sentimental writer is a mixture of the comic and the humorous. Parson Adams is a creation of humour. But both the conception and the presentation of Alceste and of Tartuffe, of Célimène and Philaminte, are purely comic, addressed to the intellect: there is no humour in them, and they refresh the

[1] The exclamation of Lady Booby, when Joseph defends himself: *'Your virtue!* I shall never survive it!'* etc., is another instance. — Joseph Andrews. Also that of Miss Mathews in her narrative to Booth : 'But such are the friendships of women.' — Amelia.

intellect they quicken to detect their comedy, by force of the contrast they offer between themselves and the wiser world about them; that is to say, society, or that assemblage of minds whereof the Comic spirit has its origin.

Byron had splendid powers of humour, and the most poetic satire that we have example of, fusing at times to hard irony. He had no strong comic sense, or he would not have taken an anti-social position, which is directly opposed to the Comic; and in his philosophy, judged by philosophers, he is a comic figure, by reason of this deficiency. 'Sobald er philosophirt ist er ein Kind,' Goethe says of him. Carlyle sees him in this comic light, treats him in the humorous manner.

The Satirist is a moral agent, often a social scavenger, working on a storage of bile.

The Ironeïst is one thing or another, according to his caprice. Irony is the humour of satire; it may be savage as in Swift, with a moral object, or sedate, as in Gibbon, with a malicious. The foppish irony fretting to be seen, and the irony which leers, that you shall not mistake its intention, are failures in satiric effort pretending to the treasures of ambiguity.

The Humourist of mean order is a refreshing laugher, giving tone to the feelings and sometimes allowing the feelings to be too much for him. But the humourist of high has an embrace of contrasts beyond the scope of the Comic poet.

Heart and mind laugh out at Don Quixote, and still you brood on him. The juxtaposition of the knight and squire is a Comic conception, the opposition of their natures most humorous. They are as different as the two hemispheres in the time of Columbus, yet they touch and are bound in one by laughter. The knight's great aims and constant mishaps, his chivalrous valiancy exercised on absurd objects, his good sense along the highroad of the craziest of expeditions; the compassion he plucks out

of derision, and the admirable figure he pre-
serves while stalking through the frantically
grotesque and burlesque assailing him, are in
the loftiest moods of humour, fusing the
Tragic sentiment with the Comic narrative.

The stroke of the great humourist is world-
wide, with lights of Tragedy in his laughter.

Taking a living great, though not creative,
humourist to guide our description: the skull
of Yorick is in his hands in our seasons of
festival; he sees visions of primitive man
capering preposterously under the gorgeous
robes of ceremonial. Our souls must be on
fire when we wear solemnity, if we would not
press upon his shrewdest nerve. Finite and
infinite flash from one to the other with him,
lending him a two-edged thought that peeps
out of his peacefullest lines by fits, like the
lantern of the fire-watcher at windows, going
the rounds at night. The comportment and
performances of men in society are to him, by
the vivid comparison with their mortality,
more grotesque than respectable. But ask

yourself, Is he always to be relied on for justness? He will fly straight as the emissary
eagle back to Jove at the true Hero. He will
also make as determined a swift descent upon
the man of his wilful choice, whom we cannot
distinguish as a true one. This vast power of
his, built up of the feelings and the intellect
in union, is often wanting in proportion and
in discretion. Humourists touching upon
History or Society are given to be capricious.
They are, as in the case of Sterne, given to be
sentimental; for with them the feelings are
primary, as with singers. Comedy, on the
other hand, is an interpretation of the general
mind, and is for that reason of necessity kept
in restraint. The French lay marked stress on
mesure et goût, and they own how much they
owe to Molière for leading them in simple
justness and taste. We can teach them many
things; they can teach us in this.

The Comic poet is in the narrow field, or
enclosed square, of the society he depicts; and
he addresses the still narrower enclosure of

men's intellects, with reference to the operation
of the social world upon their characters. He
is not concerned with beginnings or endings or
surroundings, but with what you are now
weaving. To understand his work and value
it, you must have a sober liking of your kind
and a sober estimate of our civilized qualities.
The aim and business of the Comic poet are
misunderstood, his meaning is not seized nor
his point of view taken, when he is accused of
dishonouring our nature and being hostile to
sentiment, tending to spitefulness and making
an unfair use of laughter. Those who detect
irony in Comedy do so because they choose to
see it in life. Poverty, says the satirist, has
nothing harder in itself than that it makes
men ridiculous. But poverty is never ridiculous to Comic perception until it attempts
to make its rags conceal its bareness in a for-
lorn attempt at decency, or foolishly to rival
ostentation. Caleb Balderstone, in his endea-
vour to keep up the honour of a noble household in a state of beggary, is an exquisitely

comic character. In the case of 'poor relatives,' on the other hand, it is the rich, whom they perplex, that are really comic; and to laugh at the former, not seeing the comedy of the latter, is to betray dulness of vision. Humourist and Satirist frequently hunt together as Ironeïsts in pursuit of the grotesque, to the exclusion of the Comic. That was an affecting moment in the history of the Prince Regent, when the First Gentleman of Europe burst into tears at a sarcastic remark of Beau Brummel's on the cut of his coat. Humour, Satire, Irony, pounce on it altogether as their common prey. The Comic spirit eyes but does not touch it. Put into action, it would be farcical. It is too gross for Comedy.

Incidents of a kind casting ridicule on our unfortunate nature instead of our conventional life, provoke derisive laughter, which thwarts the Comic idea. But derision is foiled by the play of the intellect. Most of doubtful causes in contest are open to Comic interpretation, and any intellectual pleading of

6

a doubtful cause contains germs of an Idea of Comedy.

The laughter of satire is a blow in the back or the face. The laughter of Comedy is impersonal and of unrivalled politeness, nearer a smile; often no more than a smile. It laughs through the mind, for the mind directs it; and it might be called the humour of the mind.

One excellent test of the civilization of a country, as I have said, I take to be the flourishing of the Comic idea and Comedy; and the test of true Comedy is that it shall awaken thoughtful laughter.

If you believe that our civilization is founded in common-sense (and it is the first condition of sanity to believe it), you will, when contemplating men, discern a Spirit overhead; not more heavenly than the light flashed upward from glassy surfaces, but luminous and watchful; never shooting beyond them, nor lagging in the rear; so closely attached to them that it may be taken for a slavish reflex, until its features are studied. It has the sage's brows, and the sunny malice of a faun lurks at the corners of the half-closed lips drawn in an idle wariness of half tension. That slim feasting smile, shaped like the long-bow, was once a big round satyr's laugh, that flung up the brows like a fortress lifted by gunpowder. The laugh will come again, but it will be of the order of the smile, finely tempered, showing sunlight of the mind, mental richness rather than noisy enormity. Its common aspect is one of unsolicitous observation, as if surveying a full field and having leisure to dart on its chosen morsels, without any fluttering eagerness. Men's future upon earth does not attract it; their honesty and shapeliness in the present does; and whenever they wax out of proportion, overblown, affected, pretentious, bombastical, hypocritical, pedantic, fantastically delicate; whenever it sees them self-deceived or hoodwinked, given to run riot in idolatries, drifting into vanities, congregating in absurdities, planning short-sightedly, plotting dementedly; whenever they are at variance with their professions, and violate the unwritten but perceptible laws binding them in consideration one to another; whenever they offend sound reason, fair justice; are false in humility or mined with conceit, individually, or in the bulk — the Spirit overhead will look humanely malign and cast an oblique light on them, followed by volleys of silvery laughter. That is the Comic Spirit.

Not to distinguish it is to be bull-blind to the spiritual, and to deny the existence of a mind of man where minds of men are in working conjunction.

You must, as I have said, believe that our state of society is founded in common-sense, otherwise you will not be struck by the contrasts the Comic Spirit perceives, or have it to look to for your consolation. You will, in fact, be standing in that peculiar oblique beam of light, yourself illuminated to the general eye as the very object of chase and doomed quarry of the thing obscure to you. But to feel its presence and to see it is your assurance that many sane and solid minds are with you in what you are experiencing: and this of itself spares you the pain of satirical heat, and the bitter craving to strike heavy blows. You share the sublime of wrath, that would not have hurt the foolish, but merely demonstrate their foolishness. Molière was contented to revenge himself on the critics of the École des Femmes, by writing the Critique de l'École des Femmes, one of the wisest as well as the playfullest of studies in criticism. A perception of the comic spirit gives high fellowship. You become a citizen of the selecter world, the highest we know of in connection with our old world, which is not supermundane. Look there for your unchallengeable upper class! You feel that you are one of this our civilized community, that you cannot escape from it, and would not if you could. Good hope sustains you; weariness does not overwhelm you; in isolation you see no charms for vanity; personal pride is greatly moderated. Nor shall your title of citizenship exclude you from

worlds of imagination or of devotion. The
Comic spirit is not hostile to the sweetest
songfully poetic. Chaucer bubbles with it:
Shakespeare overflows: there is a mild moon's
ray of it (pale with super-refinement through
distance from our flesh and blood planet) in
Comus. Pope has it, and it is the daylight
side of the night half obscuring Cowper. It
is only hostile to the priestly element, when
that, by baleful swelling, transcends and over-
laps the bounds of its office: and then, in
extreme cases, it is too true to itself to speak,
and veils the lamp: as, for example, the spectacle of Bossuet over the dead body of Molière:
at which the dark angels may, but men do not
laugh.

We have had comic pulpits, for a sign that
the laughter-moving and the worshipful may
be in alliance: I know not how far comic, or
how much assisted in seeming so by the un-
expectedness and the relief of its appearance: at
least they are popular, they are said to win the
ear. Laughter is open to perversion, like other

good things; the scornful and the brutal sorts
are not unknown to us; but the laughter
directed by the Comic spirit is a harmless
wine, conducing to sobriety in the degree that
it enlivens.   It enters you like fresh air into a
study; as when one of the sudden contrasts
of the comic idea floods the brain like reassur-
ing daylight.   You are cognizant of the true
kind by feeling that you take it in, savour it,
and have what flowers live on, natural air for
food.   That which you give out — the joyful
roar — is not the better part; let that go to
good fellowship and the benefit of the lungs.
Aristophanes promises his auditors that if they
will retain the ideas of the comic poet care-
fully, as they keep dried fruits in boxes, their
garments shall smell odoriferous of wisdom
throughout the year.   The boast will not be
thought an empty one by those who have
choice friends that have stocked themselves
according to his directions.   Such treasuries
of sparkling laughter are wells in our desert.
Sensitiveness to the comic laugh is a step in

civilization. To shrink from being an object
of it is a step in cultivation. We know the
degree of refinement in men by the matter
they will laugh at, and the ring of the laugh;
but we know likewise that the larger natures
are distinguished by the great breadth of their
power of laughter, and no one really loving
Molière is refined by that love to despise or
be dense to Aristophanes, though it may be
that the lover of Aristophanes will not have
risen to the height of Molière. Embrace them
both, and you have the whole scale of laughter
in your breast. Nothing in the world sur-
passes in stormy fun the scene in *The Frogs*,
when Bacchus and Xanthias receive their
thrashings from the hands of businesslike
Œacus, to discover which is the divinity of
the two, by his imperviousness to the mortal
condition of pain, and each, under the obliga-
tion of not crying out, makes believe that his
horrible bellow — the god's *iou iou* being the
lustier — means only the stopping of a sneeze,
or horseman sighted, or the prelude to an

invocation to some deity: and the slave con-
trives that the god shall get the bigger lot of
blows. Passages of Rabelais, one or two in
Don Quixote, and the Supper in the Manner
of the Ancients, in Peregrine Pickle, are of a
similar cataract of laughter. But it is not
illuminating; it is not the laughter of the
mind. Molière's laughter, in his purest comedies, is ethereal, as light to our nature, as
colour to our thoughts. The Misanthrope and
the Tartuffe have no audible laughter; but
the characters are steeped in the comic spirit.
They quicken the mind through laughter, from
coming out of the mind; and the mind accepts
them because they are clear interpretations of
certain chapters of the Book lying open before
us all. Between these two stand Shakespeare
and Cervantes, with the richer laugh of heart
and mind in one; with much of the Aristophanic robustness, something of Molière's
delicacy.

The laughter heard in circles not pervaded

by the Comic idea, will sound harsh and soulless, like versified prose, if you step into them with a sense of the distinction. You will fancy you have changed your habitation to a planet remoter from the sun. You may be among powerful brains too. You will not find poets — or but a stray one, over-worshipped. You will find learned men undoubtedly, professors, reputed philosophers, and illustrious dilettanti. They have in them, perhaps, every element composing light, except the Comic. They read verse, they discourse of art; but their eminent faculties are not under that vigilant sense of a collective supervision, spiritual and present, which we have taken note of. They build a temple of arrogance; they speak much in the voice of oracles; their hilarity, if it does not dip in grossness, is usually a form of pugnacity.

Insufficiency of sight in the eye looking outward has deprived them of the eye that should look inward. They have never weighed themselves in the delicate balance of the Comic idea so as to obtain a suspicion of the rights and dues of the world; and they have, in consequence, an irritable personality. A very learned English professor crushed an argument in a political discussion, by asking his adversary angrily: 'Are you aware, sir, that I am a philologer?'

The practice of polite society will help in training them, and the professor on a sofa with beautiful ladies on each side of him, may become their pupil and a scholar in manners without knowing it : he is at least a fair and pleasing spectacle to the Comic Muse. But the society named polite is volatile in its adorations, and to-morrow will be petting a bronzed soldier, or a black African, or a prince, or a spiritualist : ideas cannot take root in its ever-shifting soil. It is besides addicted in self-defence to gabble exclusively of the affairs of its rapidly revolving world, as children on a whirligoround bestow their attention on the wooden horse or cradle ahead of them, to escape from giddiness and preserve a notion

of identity. The professor is better out of
a circle that often confounds by lionizing,
sometimes annoys by abandoning, and always
confuses. The school that teaches gently
what peril there is lest a cultivated head should
still be coxcomb's, and the collisions which may
befall high-soaring minds, empty or full, is
more to be recommended than the sphere of
incessant motion supplying it with material.

Lands where the Comic spirit is obscure
overhead are rank with raw crops of matter.
The traveller accustomed to smooth highways
and people not covered with burrs and prickles
is amazed, amid so much that is fair and
cherishable, to come upon such curious bar-
barism. An Englishman paid a visit of
admiration to a professor in the Land of Cul-
ture, and was introduced by him to another
distinguished professor, to whom he took so
cordially as to walk out with him alone one
afternoon. The first professor, an erudite
entirely worthy of the sentiment of scholarly
esteem prompting the visit, behaved (if we

exclude the dagger) with the vindictive jealousy of an injured Spanish beauty. After a short prelude of gloom and obscure explosions, he discharged upon his faithless admirer the bolts of passionate logic familiar to the ears of flighty caballeros:—'Either I am a fit object of your admiration, or I am not. Of these things one—either you are competent to judge, in which case I stand condemned by you; or you are incompetent, and therefore impertinent, and you may betake yourself to your country again, hypocrite!' The admirer was for persuading the wounded scholar that it is given to us to be able to admire two professors at a time. He was driven forth.

Perhaps this might have occurred in any country, and a comedy of *The Pedant*, discovering the greedy humanity within the dusty scholar, would not bring it home to one in particular. I am mindful that it was in Germany, when I observe that the Germans have gone through no comic training to warn them of the sly, wise emanation eyeing them

from aloft, nor much of satirical. Heinrich
Heine has not been enough to cause them to
smart and meditate. Nationally, as well as
individually, when they are excited they are in
danger of the grotesque, as when, for instance,
they decline to listen to evidence, and raise a
national outcry because one of German blood
has been convicted of crime in a foreign
country. They are acute critics, yet they still
wield clubs in controversy. Compare them in
this respect with the people schooled in La
Bruyère, La Fontaine, Molière; with the
people who have the figures of a Trissotin and
a Vadius before them for a comic warning of
the personal vanities of the caressed professor.
It is more than difference of race. It is the
difference of traditions, temper, and style,
which comes of schooling.

The French controversialist is a polished
swordsman, to be dreaded in his graces and
courtesies. The German is Orson, or the mob,
or a marching army, in defence of a good case
or a bad — a big or a little. His irony is a

missile of terrific tonnage : sarcasm he emits
like a blast from a dragon's mouth. He must
and will be Titan. He stamps his foe under-
foot, and is astonished that the creature is not
dead, but stinging; for, in truth, the Titan is
contending, by comparison, with a god.

When the Germans lie on their arms,
looking across the Alsatian frontier at the
crowds of Frenchmen rushing to applaud
L'ami Fritz at the Théâtre Français, looking
and considering the meaning of that applause,
which is grimly comic in its political response
to the domestic moral of the play — when the
Germans watch and are silent, their force of
character tells. They are kings in music, we
may say princes in poetry, good speculators
in philosophy, and our leaders in scholarship.
That so gifted a race, possessed moreover of
the stern good sense which collects the waters
of laughter to make the wells, should show at
a disadvantage, I hold for a proof, instructive
to us, that the discipline of the comic spirit is
needful to their growth. We see what they

can reach to in that great figure of modern man-
hood, Goethe. They are a growing people;
they are conversable as well; and when their
men, as in France, and at intervals at Berlin
tea-tables, consent to talk on equal terms with
their women, and to listen to them, their
growth will be accelerated and be shapelier.
Comedy, or, in any form the Comic spirit, will
then come to them to cut some figures out of
the block, show them the mirror, enliven and
irradiate the social intelligence.

Modern French comedy is commendable for
the directness of the study of actual life, as far
as that, which is but the early step in such a
scholarship, can be of service in composing
and colouring the picture. A consequence of
this crude, though well-meant, realism is the
collision of the writers in their scenes and
incidents, and in their characters. The Muse
of most of them is an *Aventurière*. She is
clever, and a certain diversion exists in the
united scheme for confounding her. The
object of this person is to reinstate herself in

the decorous world; and either, having accomplished this purpose through deceit, she has a *nostalgie de la boue*, that eventually casts her back into it, or she is exposed in her course of deception when she is about to gain her end. A very good, innocent young man is her victim, or a very astute, goodish young man obstructs her path. This latter is enabled to be the champion of the decorous world by knowing the indecorous well. He has assisted in the progress of Aventurières downward; he will not help them to ascend. The world is with him; and certainly it is not much of an ascension they aspire to; but what sort of a figure is he? The triumph of a candid realism is to show him no hero. You are to admire him (for it must be supposed that realism pretends to waken some admiration) as a credibly living young man; no better, only a little firmer and shrewder, than the rest. If, however, you think at all, after the curtain has fallen, you are likely to think that the Aventurières have a case to plead against him.

7

True, and the author has not said anything
to the contrary; he has but painted from the
life; he leaves his audience to the reflections of
unphilosophic minds upon life, from the speci-
men he has presented in the bright and narrow
circle of a spy-glass.

I do not know that the fly in amber is of
any particular use, but the Comic idea enclosed
in a comedy makes it more generally perceptible and portable, and that is an advantage.
There is a benefit to men in taking the lessons
of Comedy in congregations, for it enlivens the
wits; and to writers it is beneficial, for they
must have a clear scheme, and even if they
have no idea to present, they must prove that
they have made the public sit to them before
the sitting to see the picture. And writing
for the stage would be a corrective of a too-
incrusted scholarly style, into which some great
ones fall at times. It keeps minor writers to a
definite plan, and to English. Many of them
now swelling a plethoric market, in the composition of novels, in pun-manufactories and in

journalism; attached to the machinery forcing perishable matter on a public that swallows voraciously and groans; might, with encouragement, be attending to the study of art in literature. Our critics appear to be fascinated by the quaintness of our public, as the world is when our beast-garden has a new importation of magnitude, and the creature's appetite is reverently consulted. They stipulate for a writer's popularity before they will do much more than take the position of umpires to record his failure or success. Now the pig supplies the most popular of dishes, but it is not accounted the most honoured of animals, unless it be by the cottager. Our public might surely be led to try other, perhaps finer, meat. It has good taste in song. It might be taught as justly, on the whole, and the sooner when the cottager's view of the feast shall cease to be the humble one of our literary critics, to extend this capacity for delicate choosing in the direction of the matter arousing laughter.